Who Is Elton John?

Who Is Elton John?

by Kirsten Anderson
illustrated by Joseph J. M. Qiu

Penguin Workshop

To my rock-goddess sister, Sharon,
who taught me everything about music—KA

To Sir Elton John and people who love his music—JQ

PENGUIN WORKSHOP
An Imprint of Penguin Random House LLC, New York

Published by Penguin Workshop, an imprint of Penguin Random House LLC, New York.
PENGUIN and PENGUIN WORKSHOP are trademarks of Penguin Books Ltd.
WHO HQ & Design is a registered trademark of Penguin Random House LLC.
Printed in the USA.

Visit us online at www.penguinrandomhouse.com.

Library of Congress Control Number: 2016935029

ISBN 9780448488462 10 9 8 7 6 5 4

Contents

Who Is Elton John?

The crowd at the Troubadour club didn't pay much attention to the piano player quietly singing onstage. The twenty-three-year-old singer's record company had worked hard to get many important people in the music business to come to the Los Angeles club and hear its new discovery. But on this August night in 1970, most of the audience was much more famous than the man onstage. They talked to one another and looked to see who else would walk in the door. They weren't very interested in this plain Englishman who wore glasses. Although he wore a "rock-and-roll" T-shirt and jeans, he looked more like a salesman than a rock star.

Elton John had thought it was a mistake to come to America. He had been struggling for years in England to get people to pay attention to him. He had written songs for other performers.

He had played and sung in bands behind other singers. He had been waiting a long time for his big break. And now it seemed as if no one would ever notice him.

Suddenly, he had had enough. All the frustration from his years of being stuck in the background boiled over. He jumped up, kicked over his piano stool, and shouted, "If you won't listen, perhaps you'll bloody well listen to this."

He started playing again, standing at the piano. But this time he pounded away at the keys. He sang loudly and confidently. It was the way he had pictured himself performing when he was a little boy in England, listening to American rock and roll on the radio.

And the audience paid attention. They heard blues, gospel, rock, and country music. Each song told its own fantastic story. Everyone knew they were hearing something special.

By the end of the night, there was a line of people waiting to get backstage to meet Elton. After years of hard work, Elton John had become an overnight success.

Chapter 1
Piano Boy

Reginald Kenneth Dwight was born in Pinner, a suburb of London, on March 25, 1947. His parents were Stanley and Sheila Dwight.

Stanley was an officer in the Royal Air Force. He was a very strict and serious man. Stanley was often away from Pinner, traveling around the world for the Royal Air Force. Reggie was mostly raised by his cheerful, fun-loving mother and her family.

Sheila always had music playing in the house. One day, when Reggie was just a toddler, he climbed onto the piano bench and played a song he had heard on the radio. Young Reggie could play other songs, too, just by listening to them.

He began to take piano lessons with a teacher in Pinner when he was seven.

Stanley Dwight cared about other things. He wanted Reggie to be neat, polite, and obedient, like the soldiers he commanded. Reggie tried to please his father as much as he could, but Stanley made him nervous.

Reggie only felt comfortable with Stanley at football matches. *Football* is what people outside of the United States call soccer.

Football fans in Britain are very devoted to their teams, and football matches are always big news. Reggie was a huge fan of his local team, Watford Football Club. Stanley and Reggie went to see them play whenever they could.

When Reggie was eleven, he was accepted into a program at the Royal Academy of Music.

ROYAL ACADEMY OF MUSIC IN LONDON

Every Saturday he took the train to London for his lessons. He studied classical music by composers from the eighteenth and nineteenth centuries, such as Bach, Mozart, and Beethoven.

Reggie practiced all the classical pieces his teachers gave him, but his heart wasn't in them. He was much more interested in the new rock-and-roll music that became popular in the 1950s. Stanley hated it. But Sheila bought Elvis Presley records and played them when Stanley wasn't home.

Reggie's favorite rock stars were Little Richard and Jerry Lee Lewis. They didn't sit on a piano bench calmly playing. They jumped up, kicked the bench over, and pounded the keyboard until the piano shook. Reggie dreamed of being up onstage, playing and singing just like them.

It would have been hard for anyone to imagine that. Adults thought Reggie was a quiet child with excellent manners. Kids didn't notice him much. He was just that shy, chubby boy who always seemed to be on his way to a piano lesson.

GIMME A BEAT

WHAT MADE ROCK AND ROLL DIFFERENT THAN THE MUSIC YOUNG PEOPLE LISTENED TO AND DANCED TO IN THE 1920S, '30S, AND '40S? BORN FROM GOSPEL MUSIC AND RHYTHM AND BLUES POPULAR IN AFRICAN AMERICAN COMMUNITIES, ROCK AND ROLL WAS PLAYED LOUDER AND FASTER THAN OTHER FORMS OF POPULAR MUSIC.

ONE OF THE BIGGEST DIFFERENCES WAS THE BEAT. MOST POPULAR MUSIC BEFORE THE 1950S SOUNDED LIKE THIS: DA da DA da. IT'S A VERY CALM, EVEN BEAT. BUT ROCK MUSIC WENT LIKE THIS: da DA da DA da DA. IT'S FASTER AND COOLER, EVEN WHEN SPOKEN. ROCK AND ROLL: IT'S ALL ABOUT THE BEAT.

Reggie loved collecting new music. But he didn't listen to his albums, he studied them. He memorized the names of producers and musicians. He learned the names of songwriters and music publishers. When Stanley and Sheila fought, Reggie went to his room to study his record collection. He became an expert on the songs and styles of Elvis, Little Richard, and Jerry Lee Lewis.

LITTLE RICHARD AND JERRY LEE LEWIS

RICHARD WAYNE PENNIMAN GOT THE NICKNAME "LIL' RICHARD" BECAUSE HE WAS SO SMALL AND SKINNY. HE DEVELOPED HIS SINGING STYLE WITH GOSPEL MUSIC AT HIS CHURCH, AND HE STARTED TO SING PROFESSIONALLY WITH TOURING GOSPEL GROUPS WHEN HE WAS A TEENAGER. LITTLE RICHARD HAD HIS FIRST BIG HIT, "TUTTI FRUTTI," IN 1955 AND BECAME KNOWN FOR HIS HIGH-ENERGY LIVE SHOWS AND THE FANCY CLOTHES AND MAKEUP HE WORE ONSTAGE.

JERRY LEE LEWIS ALSO BEGAN PLAYING PIANO AT A YOUNG AGE. DURING ONE SHOW, HE ACCIDENTALLY KICKED THE PIANO BENCH OVER, AND THE AUDIENCE RESPONDED SO WELL THAT HE MADE IT PART OF HIS ACT. JERRY LEE GOT HIS BIG BREAK IN 1957 WITH THE HIT SONGS "WHOLE LOTTA SHAKIN' GOIN' ON" AND "GREAT BALLS OF FIRE." HE WAS NICKNAMED "THE KILLER" FOR THE WAY HE POUNDED THE KEYS OF THE PIANO AND SHOUTED HIS SONGS.

In 1962, Reggie's parents divorced. Stanley Dwight moved away and remarried. He began a new family with his new wife. He rarely came back to Pinner.

Reggie was both relieved and sad. He was happy to not hear his parents fighting anymore, but he felt that he might have been part of the problem. He never seemed to be able to please his father. He wondered if his father even liked him very much. And he knew Stanley did not agree with his dream of becoming a musician.

Chapter 2
Backup Singer

In high school, kids discovered that Reggie could be very funny. He began to make more friends. He also began to show off his musical talent. He played classical pieces for school concerts. But after classes, he would play rock and roll for the other students.

He pounded the keys like Jerry Lee Lewis and jumped up and down like Little Richard. Kids were astonished by how good he was.

Like most teenagers in the mid-1960s, Reggie adored the Beatles. The four Beatles had quickly gone from playing small clubs in their hometown of Liverpool to being the biggest rock stars in the world. Reggie thought they always seemed to be having fun onstage. He also noticed that they wrote their own songs. Most popular singers at that time sang songs that had been written for them.

After her divorce, Reggie's mother began to date a man named Fred Farebrother. Fred was the opposite of Stanley. He was fun and relaxed. Reggie called him "Derf," *Fred* spelled backward.

When Reggie was fifteen, Derf got him a job playing piano at a hotel on Saturday nights. Reggie really wanted to be in a rock band, though.

He and some friends formed a band called the Corvettes, but it quickly fell apart. Then he joined another band. They planned to play blues music—the American music that had influenced early rock and roll. They called the band Bluesology.

Reggie decided to leave school when he was seventeen, before he graduated. He got a job at a music publisher's office. His father didn't approve. He didn't think music was a good career choice. But Reggie knew what he wanted to do.

His job at Mills Music in London wasn't very interesting. He spent his day getting tea for people and running errands. But it was exciting to be in a building where the latest music was played all the time.

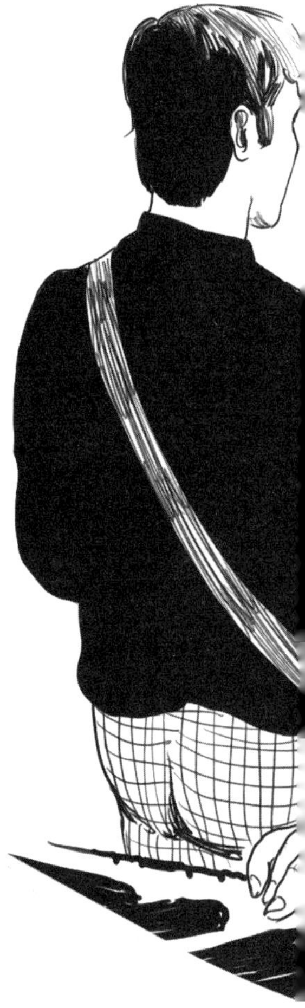

Reggie continued to perform with Bluesology on weekends. He wanted to be the band's singer. But that job went to a handsome young guitarist named Stu Brown. He looked more like a rock singer than Reggie, the chubby pianist with glasses. Reggie sang the background parts.

When Bluesology was hired to be the backup band for some American singing stars, Reggie quit his job at Mills Music to tour. Traveling all the time was hard, but the band got

the chance to play with famous singers like Patti LaBelle, the Drifters, and the Ink Spots.

A British blues singer named Long John Baldry heard Bluesology and hired them to be his band. Long John sang the lead and Stu Brown was the main backup singer. Reggie played the organ in the band. He never got the chance to sing. Reggie was losing hope and confidence. He knew he didn't look like a rock star. He was overweight and already losing his hair. He wondered if he might have better luck as a songwriter instead of as a performer. He knew he could write music, but he wasn't very good at writing the words.

One day in 1967, Reggie saw an advertisement in a newspaper. Liberty Records wanted to hear from "Artistes/Composers/Singers/Musicians to Form [a] New Group." Reggie auditioned for Ray Williams at Liberty Records.

Ray thought there was something special about the young man at the piano. Reggie told Ray that he wrote music, but not lyrics. Ray remembered another letter he had gotten in response to the ad. It was from a young man who wrote poetry that he thought could be lyrics. But he didn't write music. His name was Bernie Taupin.

Chapter 3
Partners

Bernie Taupin was seventeen, three years younger than Reggie. He had grown up in Lincolnshire, a county north of London. Lincolnshire was filled with rolling green hills and farms. It was very different than Pinner, the London suburb where Reggie grew up. Bernie described the two of them as "town mouse and country mouse."

Bernie loved poetry and stories about mythical lands, with forests full of fairies and elves, and castles with knights in shining armor. He was fascinated by stories about cowboys and the American West. He poured all his ideas about these things into fantastic poems.

Bernie came to London to meet Reggie. They were both shy young men, but they liked each other immediately. Like Reggie, Bernie also knew every popular song. They agreed that they would try to write together. Bernie gave Reggie some of his poems and returned to Lincolnshire.

Reggie sat down at the piano and wrote music to match Bernie's poems. He made recordings of the songs and mailed them back to Bernie. Then Bernie sent more poems to Reggie, who wrote music for them as well. They rarely met in person.

Reggie occasionally worked for another music publisher, Dick James Music (DJM). He played the piano and sometimes sang on demos, or simple recorded demonstrations of new songs. Stephen James of DJM heard Reggie's recordings of his and Bernie's songs. He liked the songs and put them both under contract to write songs for DJM.

Elton was thrilled because DJM was famous for publishing the Beatles' songs.

Reggie was finally going to get a chance to be a singer. He was excited, but worried. He took his mother's diet pills to lose weight. He even decided to change his name. He took the name Elton from Elton Dean, one of his bandmates in Bluesology. And he added John from John Baldry. From now on, Reggie Dwight would be known as Elton John.

And Elton was planning another big change. He got engaged to a young woman named Linda Woodrow. They had met while he was touring with Bluesology. Linda came from a very wealthy family. She had her own apartment in London, and Elton moved in with her. Bernie moved in as well.

No one thought the engagement was a good idea. Linda and Elton didn't seem to have much in common. She didn't even think he could or should become a rock star.

Elton and Bernie tried to write the kind of love songs that were popular in the late 1960s. A few of them were actually recorded by famous singers. Elton recorded one himself called "I've Been Loving You." It was released as his first solo single. But radio stations didn't play it, and few people bought it.

Elton and Bernie also kept on working on the kinds of songs they liked. These always used Bernie's complicated poems about elves, teddy bears, cowboys, and pigeons.

Elton and Linda continued to make wedding plans, but everyone could see he wasn't happy. One night John Baldry and some other friends convinced Elton that he should break up with Linda. He knew they were right. He went home and told Linda the wedding was off. She was very angry.

SPIN THAT DISK

FOR MOST OF THE TWENTIETH CENTURY, PEOPLE BOUGHT MUSIC ON HARD VINYL (PLASTIC) RECORDS. POPULAR SONGS WERE OFTEN SOLD AS "SINGLES." THESE WERE SMALL SEVEN-INCH DISKS THAT HAD THE HIT SONG ON THE "A SIDE" AND AN EXTRA SONG ON THE "B SIDE."

THE MUSIC CHARTS KEPT TRACK OF THE BEST-SELLING SINGLES EACH WEEK. IN BRITAIN, THE TOP 100 SONGS ARE LISTED ON THE UK SINGLES CHARTS. IN THE UNITED STATES, THE LIST IS MADE BY *BILLBOARD* MAGAZINE AND CALLED THE BILLBOARD HOT 100.

Elton called Sheila, who sent Derf to London to pick up Elton and Bernie. They moved back into Elton's boyhood home in Pinner with Sheila and Derf.

They shared Elton's old room and worked on their songs. Bernie wrote poems in the bedroom.

Then he would bring them to Elton in the living room. Elton sat at the piano, read them, and wrote a tune for each poem. Bernie never told Elton what a song should sound like, and Elton rarely made changes to Bernie's words. Somehow they just fit together.

Chapter 4
Rock Star

One day a new executive at Dick James Music listened to Elton and Bernie's songs. Steve Brown liked the songs they wrote to please themselves much better than the more ordinary love songs they tried to write to be popular. He suggested that from now on they should just write music in their own unique style.

The record company decided it was time for Elton to record a whole album. *Empty Sky* was released in June 1969.

Elton performed a few concerts to promote the album. He hoped to get people to listen to the songs. But he didn't perform the way he had dreamed about when he was young. He didn't pound the keys of the piano or jump up and down. Instead, he played quietly. He barely looked at the audience. *Empty Sky* didn't sell well.

Even so, Steve Brown wanted Elton to record another album. They went to a bigger, fancier studio than the small one at DJM. They brought in a music arranger who helped a whole group of musicians play Elton's piano melodies. Gus Dudgeon, a well-known producer, worked hard to make everything sound just right. This all made Elton feel more sure of himself.

This album was called simply *Elton John*. It was released in 1970. It sold well enough to earn a place on the British album charts. Elton was even asked to perform a song on the popular British TV show *Top of the Pops*. But this still didn't make him a star.

The record company executives decided to send Elton to the United States. They booked him at the Troubadour club in Los Angeles. While the band and Bernie toured the city, Elton stayed alone in the hotel. He became more and more nervous.

When the others returned to the hotel, he said he didn't want to perform. Everyone had to talk Elton into doing the shows.

Amazingly, Elton's four shows at the Troubadour were a huge hit. He became more confident each night. One day he visited Disneyland. He bought some Mickey Mouse ears and wore them onstage that night. The audience seemed to like the ears.

Elton did, too. He began to dress up more onstage, wearing boots with green wings on them and short-shorts another night.

Radio stations across the United States began to play Elton and Bernie's songs. All over America people listened to Elton John sing "Your Song," a heartfelt love song.

When Elton returned to England, people were beginning to notice him. He released his third album, called *Tumbleweed Connection*. The lyrics Bernie had written for the album were all about the American West and cowboys.

In late 1970, Elton went back to the United States for a big tour. He was even more popular in the United States than he was at home. He played shows in Boston, Philadelphia, Santa Monica, San Francisco, and New York. This time he was ready. He wore all kinds of costumes onstage—top hats, high-heeled boots, silver boots, velvet capes, purple tights, giant sunglasses. Elton knew he would never be a tall, thin, long-haired rock star, so why not just be himself, only sillier?

Onstage Elton pounded the piano keys, doing back kicks as he played, singing confidently to the audience. Offstage, though, he was still shy. He couldn't believe that someone like Bob Dylan, the singer-songwriter who many considered the great poet of the 1960s, wanted to meet him.

At last, Elton was a famous pop star. "Your Song" was a hit in both the United States and Britain. His album was selling well. When he got home, he bought an apartment in London. John Reid, a young Scottish record executive, moved in with him.

Elton had met John on his first visit to the United States. John knew all about the music world. He was organized, businesslike, and tough. He was everything Elton needed, both in his career and at home. They fell in love. And John became Elton's manager.

Chapter 5
Captain Fantastic

During the early 1970s, Elton and Bernie wrote some of their greatest hits. The songs "Rocket Man," about an unhappy astronaut, and "Daniel," about a Vietnam War veteran, were big hits. "Crocodile Rock" became Elton's first song to reach number one in the United States.

There weren't many other piano-playing rock stars. No one else sounded like Elton. No one else played in so many different styles. No one else put on a show like Elton either. He seemed to always be having a good time onstage.

In 1973, Elton released his biggest album yet. He and Bernie wrote and recorded twenty-one songs in just twelve days. *Goodbye Yellow Brick Road* went to number one on the US and British album charts and produced many hit songs, including the title song, "Saturday Night's Alright for Fighting," "Candle in the Wind," and "Bennie and the Jets."

Elton and John Reid formed Rocket Record Company, a new record label, in 1973. They planned to use the company to develop new talent.

One of Elton's favorite Rocket artists was Kiki Dee, a singer from northern England whose voice he loved.

Elton also became vice-president of his beloved Watford Football Club in 1973. One of his managers knew some of the club's board members. He told them Elton was a big fan and would love to be involved. The club was struggling at the time, and Elton was thrilled to have a chance to help.

Elton's 1975 album was called *Captain Fantastic and the Brown Dirt Cowboy*. It told the story of Elton and Bernie's years together. Elton was Captain Fantastic, and Bernie was the cowboy. The hit song "Someone Saved My Life Tonight"

was about the night friends talked Elton out of marrying Linda. This song was very different for Elton. Usually the words he sang expressed Bernie's feelings and memories. This time, though, he was singing about himself and his own life.

In 1975, a popular British rock band named The Who made a film based on their album *Tommy*. Elton played a character called the Pinball Wizard. He only appeared in one scene, but he got to record his own version of the album's most famous song, "Pinball Wizard." It became another big hit for Elton.

Elton had become very rich. He bought a country house outside of London. The record collection he'd started when he was young now filled an entire room. Elton bought paintings, statues, furniture, and jewelry. But he didn't spend all his money on himself. Elton helped family members and friends start their own businesses and find jobs. He even got back in touch with his father. Elton visited Stanley Dwight and his second wife. He brought them gifts and played football with their four sons.

Each of Elton's concert tours became bigger and bigger. Elton made grand entrances. He walked down glimmering staircases. Rows of piano lids spelled out his name, and white doves flew into the air. His costumes were covered with rhinestones, feathers, and sparkles.

TOMMY

IN 1969, THE WHO RELEASED AN ALBUM CALLED *TOMMY*. PETE TOWNSHEND, THE BAND'S LEAD GUITARIST AND MAIN SONGWRITER, CALLED IT A "ROCK OPERA" BECAUSE ALL THE SONGS CONNECTED TO TELL A STORY.

TOMMY IS A BOY WHO CANNOT SEE, HEAR, OR SPEAK. WHEN HE BECOMES A TEENAGER, HE DISCOVERS THAT HE HAS A TALENT FOR THE ARCADE GAME PINBALL. HE BECOMES A PINBALL CHAMPION AND IS SUDDENLY CURED. HE CAN SEE, SPEAK, AND HEAR. HE PREACHES ABOUT HOW HE CURED HIMSELF AND WINS THOUSANDS OF FOLLOWERS. BUT HIS SUCCESS IS SHORT-LIVED.

THE WHO ORIGINALLY PERFORMED *TOMMY* AS A CONCERT. IN 1975, THE MOVIE VERSION WAS RELEASED. A STAGE MUSICAL VERSION OF *TOMMY* OPENED ON BROADWAY IN 1993, AND IT WON SEVERAL TONY AWARDS.

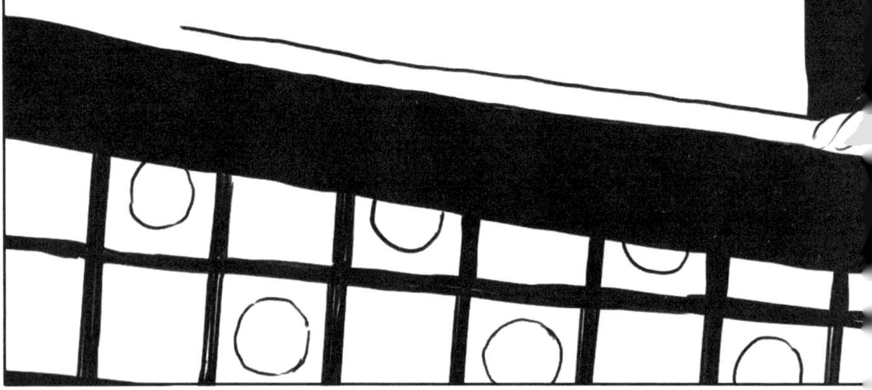

He played a concert at Dodger Stadium in Los Angeles dressed in a baseball uniform covered in glittering rhinestones. He wore giant glasses in all

LA
Dodgers
1

different shapes and colors, with frames that lit up and blinked. He sometimes dyed his hair orange or green. He became known for wearing boots with enormous platforms and high heels. He was a rock star.

Celebrities like Elizabeth Taylor, Diana Ross, and Cher came to Elton's concerts and visited backstage. He became friends with other rock stars like the Rolling Stones, Queen, and Rod Stewart.

GLAM ROCK

ELTON WAS NOT THE ONLY MUSICIAN DRESSING UP IN THE EARLY 1970S. ACTUALLY, HE FIT INTO A NEW STYLE OF MUSIC KNOWN AS GLAM ROCK, SOMETIMES CALLED "GLITTER ROCK." GLAMOROUS ROCKERS WERE THE OPPOSITE OF THE T-SHIRT-AND-JEANS-WEARING PERFORMERS OF THE LATE 1960S. THEY WORE SHINY JUMPSUITS, HIGH-HEELED SHOES, AND MAKEUP. GLAM ROCKERS PUT ON WIGS AND DYED THEIR HAIR. THEY SOMETIMES LOOKED LIKE SPACE TRAVELERS FROM THE FUTURE. DAVID BOWIE DRESSED AS AN ALIEN AND SAID HE WAS ZIGGY STARDUST, A CHARACTER ON ONE OF HIS ALBUMS.

SOME FAMOUS GLAM-ROCK BANDS WERE T. REX, MOTT THE HOOPLE, NEW YORK DOLLS, AND ROXY MUSIC.

He loved tennis and became good friends with the tennis star Billie Jean King. He asked Bernie to write lyrics for a song for her. Bernie wrote

"Philadelphia Freedom," named after Billie Jean's tennis team. The song was a big hit.

Elton's life seemed very exciting and glamorous. But he didn't *feel* glamorous. Each show left him exhausted. His fingers were bruised and bled from pounding the piano keys. He, the band, and Bernie now traveled in a private jet, but touring was still tough. People noticed that Elton became upset about small things. He was angry if his hotel room was not perfect. He sometimes complained that no one cared about him. There were times when he didn't want to go onstage.

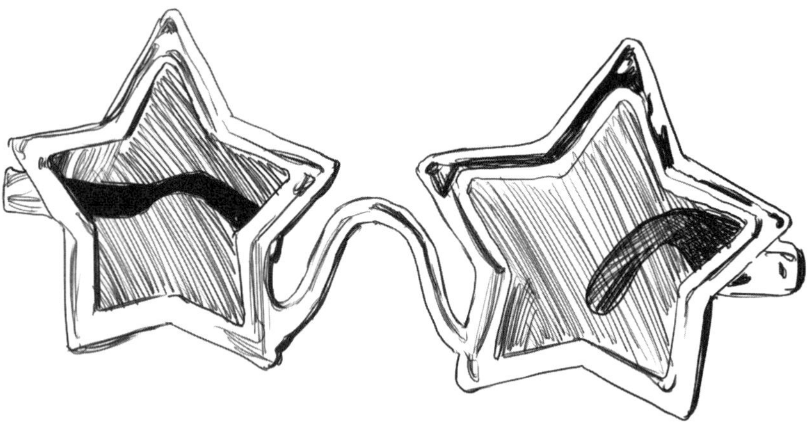

But once the show started, he seemed to be fine. He loved playing and singing. Elton said that the stage was the one place he felt at home.

Chapter 6
Goodbye Yellow Brick Road

Elton was now one of the top music stars in the world. Since his first show at the Troubadour club in 1970, he had played almost four hundred concerts in the United States, Europe, Australia,

New Zealand, and Japan. His singles and albums consistently topped the charts. In between shows and recording sessions, though, Elton sank into dark moods. He still had doubts about his talent and career.

In early 1976, Elton moved to a huge country estate in England named Woodside. He had decided to live apart from John Reid. Although they were no longer in love, John continued to manage Elton and run Rocket Record Company.

Elton filled Woodside with his records, paintings, furniture, and statues, and then shopped for more. Elton's mother, Sheila, and stepfather,

Derf, often came to visit. But Elton was alone in the big house most of the time. Sometimes he asked the housekeeper to stay and watch TV with him at night so he wouldn't feel so lonely.

Elton began to worry about turning thirty. That seemed old for a rock star. He played to thousands of fans every night, but he still felt unloved sometimes. When he was alone, he drank and used drugs to help forget his fears.

On his 1976 tour of America, he stopped wearing fancy costumes. He performed in tracksuits and sneakers. He looked like he didn't care.

That year, Elton recorded a duet with Kiki Dee. The song surprised everyone by becoming a big hit. "Don't Go Breaking My Heart," a song written by Elton and Bernie, was their first song to reach the top of the British charts.

In 1977, the only shows Elton scheduled were fund-raisers for charities. He had always cared about people and tried to help others. Now that he was a wealthy rock star, he used his music to give back as much as he could. At one of these concerts, he made a shocking announcement: This would be his last show. Elton was retiring from the concert stage.

Chapter 7
Still Standing

With no concert tours planned, Elton worked on helping his beloved Watford Football Club. He hired a new manager and gave the club money to sign better players. He even paid for improvements for the team's home stadium.

In 1978, Elton released a new album called *A Single Man*. This was the first album Elton had ever made without Bernie. Both men believed they had accomplished as much as they possibly could together. Elton's new lyrics writer was Gary Osborne. They got along well. But the magic he had with Bernie was gone.

Elton decided that he wasn't really enjoying his "retirement." He mentioned to his tour manager that he would like to perform someplace he had never been, like Russia. It was an exciting idea, but not as easy as it sounded.

In 1979, Russia was part of the Soviet Union. The Soviet government officially disapproved of rock music. Although Elton was famous all over the world, *A Single Man*, his twelfth album, was the first of his released in Russia.

Very few rock singers had performed behind the "iron curtain" of the Soviet Union, and certainly no one as famous as Elton John.

The Soviet government decided to allow Elton to do a few concerts in the cities of Moscow and Leningrad. The concerts were strange at first. Elton was used to people clapping, singing,

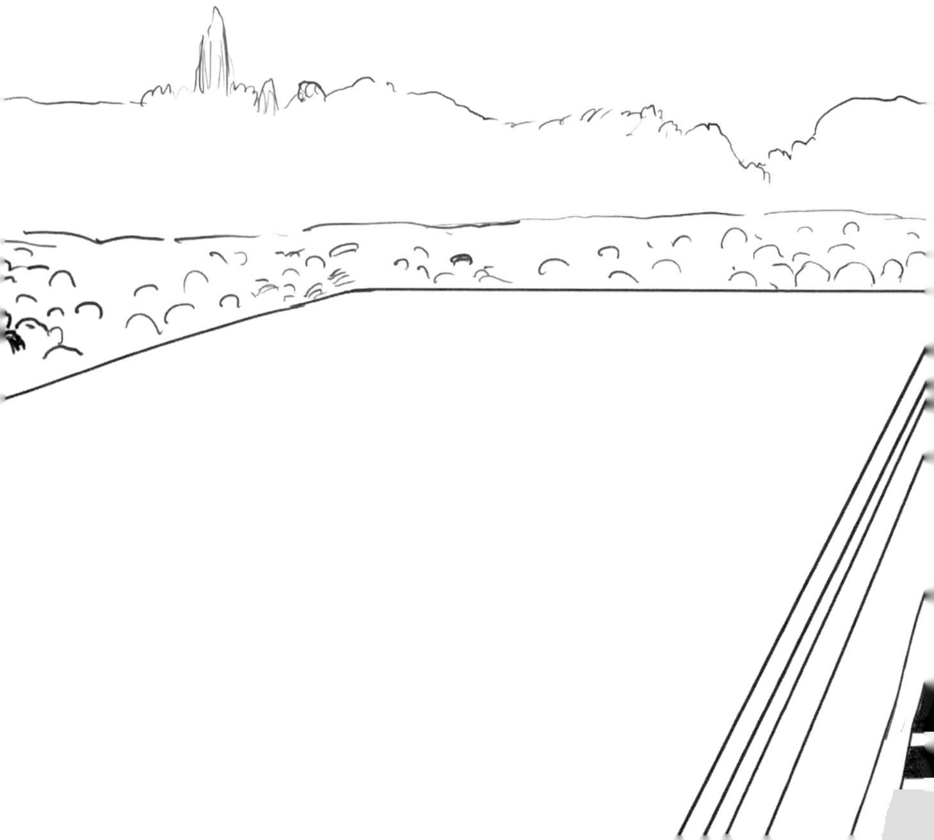

and dancing when they came to hear him perform. But the Russian audiences were very quiet. Most of them had never been to a rock concert. There were guards around the theater to keep control. But by the end of each show, the crowds warmed up. They rushed toward the stage like fans at a concert anywhere in the world.

THE IRON CURTAIN

AFTER WORLD WAR II ENDED IN 1945, NATIONS LED BY COMMUNIST GOVERNMENTS SEPARATED THEMSELVES FROM THE REST OF THE WORLD.

THE BIGGEST COMMUNIST NATION, THE UNION OF SOVIET SOCIALIST REPUBLICS, OR SOVIET UNION, CONTROLLED MOST OF THE NATIONS IN EASTERN EUROPE, INCLUDING EAST GERMANY, POLAND, AND ROMANIA. PEOPLE LIVING IN THESE COUNTRIES WORKED FOR GOVERNMENT-OWNED BUSINESSES AND SHOPPED AT GOVERNMENT-OWNED STORES.

THE SOVIETS WANTED TO KEEP NEW AND DIFFERENT IDEAS OUT OF THEIR COUNTRIES—AND ALSO KEEP THEIR CITIZENS FROM LEAVING. AFTER WORLD WAR II ENDED, THEY PUT GUARDS ON THEIR BORDERS AND SHUT OFF COMMUNICATION WITH THE REST OF THE WORLD. WINSTON CHURCHILL, THEN BRITISH PRIME MINISTER, SAID THIS WAS LIKE AN "IRON CURTAIN" FALLING BETWEEN EASTERN AND WESTERN EUROPE. AFTER THAT, PEOPLE USED THIS TERM TO DESCRIBE THE DIVIDE BETWEEN THE SOVIET UNION AND THE REST OF THE WORLD.

SOVIET
UNION
POLAND
EAST
GERMANY
CZECHOSLOVAKIA
HUNGARY
ROMANIA
BULGARIA

The success of the Russian concerts made Elton realize how much he missed being onstage. He went back to wearing costumes. And he decided to start working with Bernie again. They wrote some of their biggest hits in years: "I Guess That's Why They Call It the Blues" and "I'm Still Standing," both in 1983. Elton and Bernie were back again. And they were still standing.

Chapter 8
Reg Strikes Back

In January 1984, Elton announced that he was engaged. He planned to marry Renate Blauel, a young German woman whom Elton had met her during the recording of his last album. Renate had worked as a member of the sound-recording crew.

RENATE BLAUEL

Elton's friends and family were shocked. Since the early 1970s, they had only seen Elton date men. Society was not very accepting of gay people at that time. Elton couldn't come right out and say he was gay. Still, no one who really knew Elton expected him to marry a woman. He and Renate hadn't even known each other very long.

Elton and Renate got married on Valentine's Day in 1984 in Sydney, Australia, where Elton was touring. The couple returned to Woodside after the tour was over. But they rarely spent time together. Elton kept touring and recording. He still drank too much and used drugs. He complained and threw tantrums about silly things. Once he called his office to complain that the sound of the wind outside his hotel room was too loud. Elton later described this as a very selfish time. He said, "When I was on drugs, there was a monstrous side to me."

The other side of Elton was still a generous, caring person. In 1985, he recorded the song "That's What Friends Are For" with Stevie Wonder, Dionne Warwick, and Gladys Knight.

It was a big hit and won two Grammy awards. Profits from the song raised over $3 million to help fight the spread of the disease known as AIDS.

AIDS

AIDS STANDS FOR ACQUIRED IMMUNODEFICIENCY SYNDROME.

AT FIRST NO ONE KNEW WHAT CAUSED THE DISEASE THAT WAS KILLING SO MANY YOUNG GAY MEN, OR HOW TO PREVENT IT. MOST OF THE PEOPLE WHO GOT AIDS IN THE 1980S DIED. THEN DOCTORS DISCOVERED THAT THE HIV VIRUS WAS THE CAUSE. PEOPLE LEARNED WHAT TO DO TO AVOID IT. THERE ARE NOW MEDICINES THAT KEEP PEOPLE WITH HIV/AIDS HEALTHY ENOUGH TO LIVE WITH THE DISEASE.

Elton did a big international tour from late 1985 through the end of 1986. While on tour, he began to lose his voice. He had to cancel some shows because of it. His doctor told Elton it might be throat cancer. Elton managed to continue performing without anything seeming to be wrong.

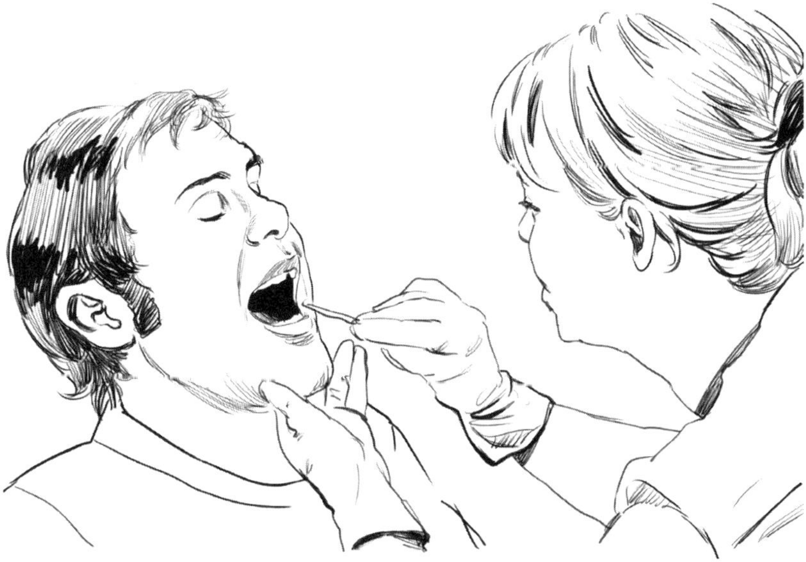

He had surgery after the tour was finished. Fortunately, it turned out that Elton did not have cancer. He just needed to rest his voice for a while.

While he was recovering in early 1987, a British newspaper called the *Sun* began to publish stories about Elton. It said that he held wild, dangerous parties with lots of drinking and drug use. Elton did drink and use drugs, but he was very quiet about it.

He never held parties like the ones the newspapers described. The stories were lies. Elton decided to sue the newspaper.

The lawsuit dragged on for months. The stories in the paper got worse and worse. It was hard on Elton. He was embarrassed for his family and friends. He spent a lot of time alone at Woodside. Everyone worried about him.

Then Elton decided it was time for some big changes. He sold all his costumes, jewelry, furniture, paintings, and statues. He sold his share of Watford Football Club. Rocket Record Company let go of all its artists except for Elton. In 1988 he released an album called *Reg Strikes Back*. The album cover showed the hats and costumes and tour props that Elton had recently sold.

Elton was ready to clean up his life and find the real Reggie Dwight. He was fighting his way back.

During this time, Elton and Renate decided to divorce. Their marriage had been a mistake. They did not have much in common and had rarely spent time together. The marriage ended quietly, and Renate moved out of Woodside.

In early December, the *Sun* gave up and settled the lawsuit. There was too much evidence to prove their stories had been made up. The newspaper made a public apology to Elton and paid him a million pounds, nearly two million US dollars. Elton donated all the money to charity. He had fought back and won.

Chapter 9
The Circle of Life

The AIDS crisis worsened throughout the 1980s. Elton spoke out about the importance of supporting people with the disease and funding research to fight it. He befriended a young American boy, Ryan White, who had gotten AIDS through a blood transfusion he had received. He flew to Indiana and was with Ryan during the last days of his life. Elton sang at Ryan's funeral.

Elton's experience with Ryan White inspired him to check into a rehab clinic and address his addictions. It was hard work, but he did it.

In 1992, he started the Elton John AIDS Foundation. Elton held a party after the 1993 Academy Awards Ceremony as a fund-raiser for the foundation. The party was a big success. It is now a yearly event that has raised many millions of dollars to help people with HIV/AIDS.

STEVEN SPIELBERG, ELTON JOHN, AND TOM HANKS

Elton hadn't had many serious relationships since he broke up with John Reid in the 1970s. Then in 1993, he met David Furnish, a Canadian advertising executive. They soon fell in love. David moved into Woodside with Elton.

Elton was hard at work writing the music for a new animated movie, *The Lion King*. Elton loved the idea of a new challenge. He wrote five songs with Tim Rice and performed the songs on the Disney movie's soundtrack.

The Lion King was released in 1994. It was a huge hit. The movie soundtrack became one of the year's top sellers. "Can You Feel the Love Tonight?" won the Academy Award for Best Original Song. A stage version of *The Lion King* opened on Broadway in 1997.

It became one of the most popular shows ever on Broadway.

Elton's career was going well. He was inducted into the Rock and Roll Hall of Fame in 1994.

He and David were very happy together. Then in 1997 he suffered two terrible losses. First his good friend Gianni Versace, the fashion designer, was murdered. Then Diana, the former Princess of Wales, died in a car accident.

Elton and Diana had known each other for years. She was also involved in the fight against AIDS.

DIANA, PRINCESS OF WALES
(1961–1997)

LADY DIANA SPENCER WAS BORN IN ENGLAND TO AN ARISTOCRATIC FAMILY. SHE BECAME THE PRINCESS OF WALES WHEN SHE MARRIED PRINCE CHARLES IN 1980. THEY HAD TWO CHILDREN, PRINCE WILLIAM AND PRINCE HARRY.

DIANA SUPPORTED MANY CHARITIES, INCLUDING THOSE THAT HELPED HOMELESS PEOPLE, DISABLED PEOPLE, DRUG ADDICTS, SICK CHILDREN, AND AIDS SUFFERERS. SHE WORKED TO PROMOTE AN INTERNATIONAL BAN ON THE CREATION AND USE OF LAND MINES. AS A PRINCESS WHO WAS SEEN AT MANY BIG EVENTS, FASHION DESIGNERS WERE ANXIOUS FOR DIANA TO WEAR THEIR CLOTHES.

JUST A YEAR AFTER HER DIVORCE FROM PRINCE CHARLES, DIANA DIED IN A CAR ACCIDENT IN PARIS.

He had often performed at events for members of the royal family, including Diana's husband Prince Charles and his brother Prince Andrew. Diana loved Elton's music. He loved her caring nature.

People all over the world were saddened by Diana's death. Thousands came to her funeral.

The royal family invited Elton to sing. He asked Bernie to rewrite the lyrics to their song "Candle in the Wind." The song had originally been written about the movie star Marilyn Monroe and how she died too young. For the funeral, Bernie changed the words to be about Diana.

Elton recorded the new version of the song. He announced that money from sales of "Candle in the Wind" would be donated to a charity that would support Diana's favorite causes. "Candle in the Wind 1997" raised millions for many charities, including the National AIDS Trust. Elton said he would never again perform the song unless Diana's sons asked him to.

Chapter 10
Your Song

In 1998, Elton became Sir Elton John when he was knighted by Queen Elizabeth II for his music and his charitable work.

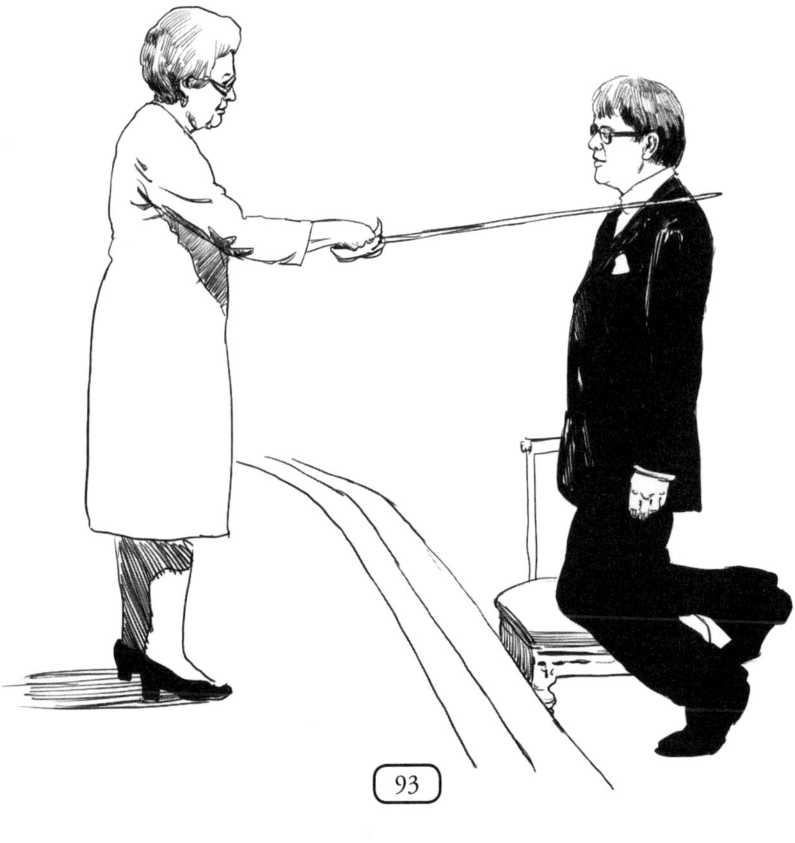

Elton and Tim Rice teamed up again to write another musical, *Aida.* Elton won a Tony award for *Aida's* music. Following that success, he was asked to write the music for a theatrical version of the movie *Billy Elliot*, about a boy who wants to be a ballet dancer. Billy has to work hard to convince his family to let him dance. Elton was happy to write the music for the show. He had loved the film.

It reminded him of his own childhood and how his father did not want him to be a musician. *Billy Elliot* opened in 2005 in London and in 2008 on Broadway.

Elton celebrated another big event in 2005. He and David entered into a civil partnership, the closest thing to marriage Britain allowed for gay couples at the time. They threw a huge party after the ceremony, with music, movie, and sports stars attending.

From 2004 to 2009, Elton performed 243 shows in Las Vegas that were called *The Red Piano*. Two years later, sixty-four-year-old Elton returned to open a new act called *Million Dollar Piano*. He played a special piano that took four years to build. It had decorations and lights scrolling across its side during the show. Elton loved performing in Las Vegas. He was happy to be able to stay in one place for weeks at a time instead of hopping on a plane every night during a tour.

Elton had a good reason for wanting to stay in one place more often. He and David had started a family. On December 25, 2010, their son Zachary Jackson Levon was born. Elton had always wanted children. Now he was finally a father.

David encouraged Elton to get into the film business. They formed Rocket Pictures, and in 2011, Rocket released *Gnomeo & Juliet*, an

animated children's movie with songs by Elton and Bernie. It was a worldwide success.

Elton and David shared more happiness in 2013. Their second son, Elijah Joseph Daniel, was born on January 11. Elton adored his growing family.

Elton had thought a civil partnership was enough for him and David. But after the birth of Zachary, he became bothered by the fact that they couldn't actually be married. He began to support the movement to make gay marriage legal. Elton said, "There is a world of difference between calling someone your 'partner' and calling them your 'husband.' 'Partner' is a word that should be preserved for people you play tennis with."

Although Elton's personal life was now busier than ever, he still was passionate about creating music. In 2013, Elton released *The Diving Board*, his thirtieth studio album. Bernie wrote the words to the songs on *The Diving Board*. Elton and Bernie still write together the same way. Bernie writes the words at his home in California, and then sends them to Elton, who sits down at the piano and writes the music. But now Bernie emails the lyrics.

Elton has described their relationship as "the strangest in pop music." Elton said, "I just go into the studio, look at the lyrics for the first time when

I put them on the piano, and go. If I haven't got it within forty minutes, I give up. It's never changed, the thrill has never gone, because I don't know what I'm going to get next. I don't know what's going to land in front of me." Captain Fantastic and the Brown Dirt Cowboy, town mouse and country mouse—they are still the perfect pair.

In 2014, Britain changed its laws to allow gay marriage. Elton and David married on December 21. Elton now had a husband and children he loved. At long last, he was happy and secure about himself, both onstage and off.

Once, shy, quiet Reggie Dwight dreamed about being famous. He looked nothing like a rock star. But he became a rock legend and so much more. He has performed all over the world and sold millions of records. And Elton's charitable work has touched as many people as his music. The Elton John AIDS Foundation has raised more than $300 million worldwide.

In 1970, people heard Elton sing "Your Song" for the first time. The song ends with Bernie's simple words: "How wonderful life is, now that you're in this world." Elton's world is finally wonderful, and he has made it that way for so many others.

TIMELINE OF ELTON JOHN'S LIFE

1947	Reginald Kenneth Dwight is born on March 25, 1947
1958	Accepted into piano program at the Royal Academy of Music
1964	Joins Bluesology
1965	Leaves school to take job at Mills Music publishing
1967	Answers talent ad from Liberty Records and is paired with poet Bernie Taupin
1969	Releases first album, *Empty Sky*
1970	Releases second album, *Elton John*, and plays concert at the Troubadour club in Los Angeles
1971	Legally changes name to Elton Hercules John
1973	*Goodbye Yellow Brick Road* reaches #7 on the British album charts, #1 in the United States
1976	Performs "Pinball Wizard" in The Who's movie *Tommy*
1979	Performs concerts in the USSR
1984	Marries Renate Blauel Performs at Live Aid event at Wembley Stadium
1988	Announces that he and Renate will divorce
1992	Starts the Elton John AIDS Foundation
1994	The movie *The Lion King* opens, with songs by Elton John and Tim Rice
1997	Plays new version of "Candle in the Wind" at the funeral for Diana, Princess of Wales; *The Lion King* opens on Broadway
2005	*Billy Elliot* opens in London
2007	Spends sixtieth birthday performing sixtieth show at Madison Square Garden
2013	Releases thirtieth studio album, *The Diving Board*
2014	Marries David Furnish

TIMELINE OF THE WORLD

World War II ends	1945
Test pilot Chuck Yeager becomes the first person to travel faster than sound	1947
George Orwell's novel *1984* is published	1949
African American Rosa Parks breaks an Alabama law by refusing to sit in the back of a city bus	1955
Elvis Presley is drafted into the US Army	1958
Andy Warhol exhibits his soup-can paintings	1962
Boxer Cassius Clay changes his name to Muhammad Ali	1964
The Green Bay Packers defeat the Kansas City Chiefs in the first Super Bowl	1967
The rock festival Woodstock takes place in Bethel, NY	1969
The United States celebrates its bicentennial	1976
The first Atari home video-gaming system is released	1977
The Sony Walkman, a portable music player with headphones, is introduced	1979
Sandra Day O'Connor becomes the first female Supreme Court Justice	1981
The Simpsons TV show premieres	1990
The Internet auction site eBay is founded	1995
Titanic becomes the first movie to earn more than $1 billion	1998
The Prius, the first mass-produced hybrid electric car, goes on sale worldwide	2000
Taipei 101, becomes the world's tallest building	2004
The iPad is introduced	2010
Selfie becomes the Oxford English Dictionary's "Word of the Year"	2013

BIBLIOGRAPHY

Buckley, David. ***Elton: The Biography.*** Chicago: Chicago Review Press, 2008.

Harper, Leah. "Elton John: The Soundtrack of My Life." ***The Guardian***, August 31, 2013, http://www.theguardian.com/music/2013/sep/01/elton-john-soundtrack-my-life.

Hillburn, Robert. "Elton John New Rock Talent." ***Los Angeles Times***, August 27, 1970, http://documents.latimes.com/aug-27-1970-elton-john-new-rock-talent/.

John, Elton. ***Love is the Cure: On Life, Loss, and the End of AIDS***. New York: Little, Brown and Co., 2012.

John, Elton. ***"A More Reflective Leap on Elton John's 'Diving Board.'" Fresh Air.*** Interviewed by Terry Gross. September 23, 2013, http://www.npr.org/templates/transcript/transcript.php?storyId=225380473.

Norman, Philip. ***Elton John.*** New York: Harmony Books, 1991.

Parker, Ian. "He's a Little Bit Funny." ***The New Yorker***, August 26, 1996.

Petridis, Alexis. "Elton John: The G2 Interview." ***The Guardian***, September 15, 2013.

Elton John: Tantrums and Tiaras. Directed by David Furnish. Rocket Pictures, 1997.

Two Rooms: A Tribute to Elton John and Bernie Taupin. Directed by Jonathan K. Bendis and Bill Richmond. The Jim Henson Company and MTV, 1991.

Websites

www.eltonjohn.com (Elton John Official Site)